Celebrations

MUSLIM FESTIVALS

Jane Cooper

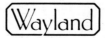

Celebrations

Christmas
Easter
Hallowe'en
Harvest

Hindu Festivals
Jewish Festivals
Muslim Festivals
New Year

All words that appear in **bold** are
explained in the glossary on page 46

First published in 1989 by
Wayland (Publishers) Limited
61 Western Road, Hove
East Sussex BN3 1JD, England

© Copyright 1989 Wayland (Publishers) Limited

British Library Cataloguing in Publication Data
Cooper, Jane
    Muslim festivals.
    1. Islamic festivals
    I. Title   II. Series
    297'.36

ISBN 1 85210 820 7

Phototypeset by Kalligraphics Limited, Horley, Surrey
Printed and bound in Italy by G. Canale & C.S.p.A., Turin

Contents

Islam

Islam is a religion followed by many people all over the world. People who follow the religion of Islam are called Muslims. They worship God. Their name for God is Allah.

Today, there are about one thousand million Muslims in the world. Most Muslims live in Africa and Asia, but many also live in Europe and the USA.

Islam lays down very clear rules about how Muslims should live their lives.

Prayers are an important part of Islam. Muslims pray to Allah five times a day. They pray in a mosque, which is a Muslim holy building.

Mosques have a minaret (a tall tower) on top. In some countries, when it is time for prayer, a man stands on the tower and calls people to the mosque.

5

These Muslim men come from many different countries. They are praying together outside a large mosque in London. They have prayer mats to kneel on. You can see that they have removed their shoes, which is something you must do when you go into a mosque.

Islam has only two main festivals. These are called
'Id al-Fitr and *'Id al-Adha*. These men are
celebrating *'Id al-Fitr*.

The Prophet Muhammad

To understand Muslim festivals, you must know something about the religion of Islam, and the **Prophet Muhammad**.

◀ All Muslims try to visit the holy city of **Mecca** at least once in their lifetime. This very old painting shows **pilgrims** travelling to Mecca.

The Prophet Muhammad taught people about Islam. He was born in AD 570, in Mecca – a town in **Arabia**. When he grew up he earned his living travelling across the desert, buying and selling goods.

Muhammad saw the way many people lived their lives and he became unhappy. He did not like to see people living badly, drinking alcohol or fighting. Sometimes he would wander into the desert on his own to think about these things.

One day Muhammad was in a cave when he was visited by the **Angel Gabriel**, who gave him messages from God. Later, these messages were written down. They became the **Qur'an**, which is the Muslim holy book. Muhammad went back to Mecca, and tried to tell people about God. But many people would not listen to him.

This is an old picture of Mecca.

All Muslim children study the holy book, the Qur'an.

After a long struggle, Muhammad left Mecca and went to the city of Medina. This journey is called the *Hijra*. In Medina he gathered followers and Islam grew. Muslims decided to begin a new **calendar**, starting with year one at the time of the *Hijra*.

Ramadan

Ramadan is a month in the Muslim calendar. It is a time of **fasting**, which means people do not eat or drink during the daytime. These people are going to the mosque to pray at dawn during *Ramadan*.

◀ During the month of *Ramadan*, people study the Qur'an and pray. There are special rules of behaviour to obey.

Ramadan is a very important time, because it was during this month that Muhammad was visited by the Angel Gabriel.

For Muslims, each new month begins when a new moon appears. There is great excitement just before the month of *Ramadan*. In some countries, people climb on to roofs and up hills to catch sight of the moon as it rises at the beginning of *Ramadan*.

During *Ramadan*, Muslims eat a light meal before dawn. Then they fast all day until sunset.

If the sky is cloudy, people cannot tell when the moon has risen, so they do not know when *Ramadan* has begun. Nowadays, Muslims listen to their radios and televisions, which tell them when the moon has been seen.

These women are praying during *Ramadan* in Britain.

Every Muslim over the age of twelve must go without food in the daytime during *Ramadan*. Only people who are sick, elderly or weak are excused. This is one of the most important duties of Muslims. Sometimes children, too, go without food and drink for a few days. If they do, they may be given presents by their relatives.

Fasting begins at dawn and ends at sunset each day. This lasts for the whole month of *Ramadan*. Muslims may not drink or smoke during the day, either.

A meal is taken before dawn each day. This meal is called *suhur*. Afterwards, people get ready to say prayers, either at a mosque or at home.

In the evening, a special meal is cooked. This is called *iftar*. These men are preparing *iftar*.

➡

Each day during *Ramadan*, fasting ends at sunset. The meal that follows, called *iftar*, is a happy time for all Muslim families.

The time of this meal is often announced on radio and television. A call is also given out from the minarets of the mosques. Muslims usually end their fast by eating a date, or drinking water. Then they pray before eating their meal.

➡

Muslims fast during *Ramadan* because they believe God (Allah) has asked them to. They believe that it teaches people to live a good life.

This Muslim lives in Mali, in Africa. He is praying during the month of *Ramadan*.

During *Ramadan*, Muslims celebrate *Lailatul Qadr*, which means Night of Power. They celebrate the night when Muhammad received the message from God through the Angel Gabriel.

Nobody knows exactly which night this was, but it was probably during the last days of *Ramadan*. During this time, some Muslims give gifts to the poor. Others spend the whole night praying in the mosque.

'Id al-Fitr

This is one of the two main festivals of the Muslim year. Prayers are said at dawn at this time.

'Id al-Fitr marks the end of *Ramadan*. Muslim families meet and give each other presents. This woman is baking bread for the 'Id feast in a clay oven in the ground.

Children dress in their best clothes to celebrate the festival of *'Id*. These children live in Saudi Arabia.

People wait eagerly to see the moon rise at the beginning of *'Id*. Again, the news of the moon rising is given out on radio and television. Muslims all around the world wait to hear the news.

20

Muslims hug each other at the 'Id festival.

Preparations for *'Id* begin long before the festival. People decorate their houses. They buy presents for each other and send special *'Id* cards.

In some Muslim countries, shops are open all night during *Ramadan*. This gives people plenty of time to shop and prepare for *'Id*.

21

In Saudi Arabia, camel races are held to celebrate the *'Id* festival.

On *'Id* day, people get up early. They have a bath and put on their best clothes. After breakfast they go to special prayer meetings. These are usually celebrated in large open places, such as parks or fields.

22

After prayers, everybody wishes each other a happy 'Id. Everyone is friendly and forgets any arguments they may have had. 'Id is a special time for children. They are given presents of sweets and new clothes.

This building is decorated with thousands of lights to celebrate 'Id.

Muslims believe it is important to help the poor. All Muslims who can afford it are expected to give money to help people in poor Muslim countries.

These men are giving money so that poor Muslims will be able to celebrate 'Id.

These Muslims live in Sierra Leone, on the west
coast of Africa. They are singing to celebrate 'Id.

In Muslim countries, people have three days of
holiday at the time of 'Id. Muslims living in other
countries take a day off work. The religion of Islam
does not allow anyone to drink alcohol or dance.
Instead, Muslims enjoy rich spicy foods and
delicious sweets.

The Hajj

Mecca is the holy city of Islam. The Prophet
Muhammad was born there. The most important
thing a Muslim can do is to visit Mecca. This holy
journey, or **pilgrimage**, is called the *Hajj*. On this
map you can see where Mecca is.

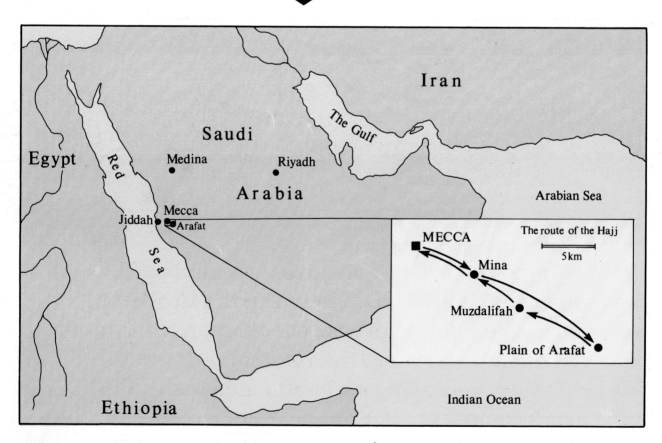

These pilgrims are going to Mecca by bus. It will be a long, hot and dusty journey. Some people save money for many years so that they can visit Mecca. All Muslims who are in good health, and can afford to go, are expected to visit Mecca once in their lives.

In the past, pilgrims travelled to Mecca on camels, horses, or even on foot. They travelled hundreds of kilometres through the hot desert.

The *Hajj* is held in the last month of the Muslim year. Sometimes this falls in winter when the weather in Mecca is cool. Sometimes it falls in summer when the weather is very hot.

Today, about two million people from all over the world go to Mecca during the time of the *Hajj*. Many travel by aeroplane. Soon the city is full up with so many pilgrims.

This pilgrim is having his hair cut on the pavement in Mecca. Cutting hair is an important part of the *Hajj* ceremonies.

Pilgrims visiting Mecca must first go to a place called *Miqat*. There they must wash, pray, and change into a special gown. This gown is called the *ihram*. It is a simple white cotton robe.

Women do not wear the *ihram*. Instead, they wear clothes that cover them all over, leaving just the face uncovered.

Many ceremonies performed during the *Hajj* come from the story of Abraham. He was a Prophet who lived about 4,000 years ago. Abraham built the holy building in Mecca called the **Ka'ba**.

There are some ceremonies that all Muslims must perform when they are taking part in the *Hajj.* ▶ One is to circle the Ka'ba seven times. People study the story of Abraham during the *Hajj*.

The Ka'ba is the cube-shaped building in the middle of this picture. Thousands of pilgrims are circling it seven times as part of the *Hajj*.

The story of Abraham tells how a **miracle** happened and a water well appeared to him near where the Ka'ba now stands. This well is called *Zamzam*. Pilgrims visit the well and drink there. They take cans of *Zamzam* water home to their families.

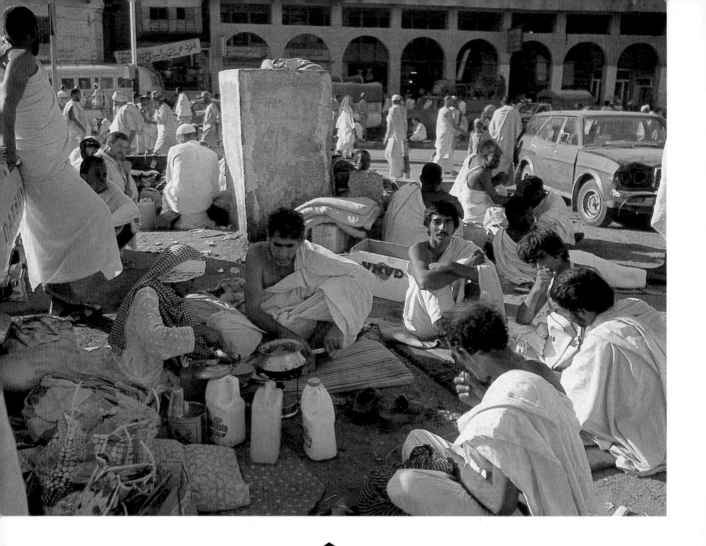

Pilgrims rest on every spare piece of pavement in Mecca during the *Hajj*.

Another *Hajj* ceremony involves throwing stones at the Pillars of Satan. This ceremony, too, comes from the story of Abraham.

Abraham dreamed that God asked him to kill his son and offer him to God. This was to test Abraham's love for God. Abraham was sad, but he agreed to do as God wished.

Then, Satan (the Devil) appeared and tried to make Abraham change his mind. He tried three times. Each time, Abraham threw stones at Satan and drove him away. During the *Hajj*, people remember this story and throw pebbles at pillars like this one.

God stopped Abraham killing his son and made him kill a sheep instead. *Hajj* pilgrims kill an animal and offer it to God in memory of Abraham's love for God.

Some pilgrims go on to visit Medina after they have been to Mecca. They visit the mosque where the Prophet Muhammad is buried.

After the five days of the *Hajj*, pilgrims return home to their families. Friends go to visit them and congratulate them on their pilgrimage. The pilgrims give their visitors *Zamzam* water to drink.

This pilgrim is praying at Mecca.

Thousands of Muslims visit the Great Mosque at Mecca during the time of the *Hajj*.

Some Muslims visit Mecca at other times of the year. They celebrate a shorter version of the ceremonies, called *'Umra*. The *Hajj* ceremonies take five days. The *'Umra* ceremonies are similar but take only a few hours to perform.

'Id al-Adha

The second great festival of Islam is called *'Id al-Adha*. It is celebrated during the month of the *Hajj*. During this festival, people give each other presents. They also kill an animal as an offering to God. This is called a **sacrifice**.

In Muslim countries, people go to market to buy a sheep, goat, cow or maybe even a camel. These shepherds in Pakistan are bringing the sheep down from the mountains in time for the *'Id al-Adha* festival.

Animals are taken to market to be sold for the
'Id al-Adha celebrations.

On the morning of the festival, people wash and put
on their best clothes. Then they say prayers
together. After this the animals are killed and
offered to God.

This young bull has been chosen as a sacrifice. It has been covered with a special cloth.

When the animal has been killed, the meat is divided into three parts. One part is given to poor people. The second part is for friends and relatives. The third part is eaten at home by the family.

Everyone has a holiday for three days. The streets in Muslim countries are full of people celebrating.

Muslims kill animals as sacrifices at this time because they are remembering the story of Abraham. They remember that he was prepared to give up his own son to God. The sacrifice of the animal reminds Muslims that they must be ready to give up their possessions, and even their own lives, if God wishes it.

When the animal is killed, it is skinned and cut up.

Other celebrations

In many Muslim countries, people celebrate important events in the history of Islam.

Milad-an-Nabi is the name given to the birthday of the Prophet Muhammad. Some Muslims celebrate this day. It is a very happy festival.

◀ These Muslims in India are celebrating the Prophet's birthday.

For Muslims, the birth of the Prophet Muhammad is one of the most important events in history.

These boys are singing in the street in the African country of Kenya. They are celebrating Muhammad's birthday.

In many parts of the world, Muslims hold parades in honour of Muhammad's birthday. Sometimes celebrations go on for a whole month. People think about the life of the Prophet Muhammad. They remember his sufferings and his struggles.

These boys in Pakistan are celebrating with colourful flags and banners.

Lailatul Bara'at means Night of Forgiveness. This takes place in the month before *Ramadan*. Muslims offer extra prayers during the night of *Lailatul Bara'at*. They ask to be forgiven for what they have done wrong. Many Muslims stay awake all through this night. Women prepare special food and children are given extra pocket money.

42

Lailatul Mi'raj means Night of Ascent. This is when people celebrate the night Muhammad went up to heaven. On this night, Muslims meet and discuss the life of Muhammad.

'Ashura takes place in the first month of the Muslim year. It was a holy day long before Islam began. On this day many Muslims fast. Some people hold parades in the streets.

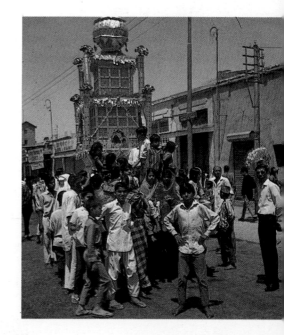

Muharram is the Muslim New Year's Day. People greet each other and think about the life of the Prophet Muhammad.

Many children take part in parades during Muslim festivals. These children live in India. They are riding through the street on a decorated cart to celebrate the *'Ashura* festival.

The Islamic Calendar

The Muslim year is shorter than the Christian year. This chart shows you when the Muslim festivals are held.

Muslim months	Muslim festivals
Muharram	*Muharram* (New Year) *'Ashura*
Safar	
Rabi 'al-Awwal	Prophet's birthday
Rabi 'al-Akhir	
Jumada' al-Ula	
Jumada' al-Akhirah	
Rajab	Night of Ascent
Sha'baan	Night of Forgiveness
Ramadan	Fast of *Ramadan* Night of Power
Shawwal	*'Id al-Fitr*
Dhul-Qi'dah	
Dhul-Hijjah	The *Hajj* *'Id al-Adha*

Glossary

Angel Gabriel   The angel who brought God's message to Muhammad.

Arabia   The country where the Prophet Muhammad was born. It is now called Saudi Arabia.

Calendar   A system for dividing the year into different months.

Fasting   Giving up eating and drinking.

Ka'ba   The cube-shaped building in the Great Mosque in Mecca.

Mecca   The Muslim holy city, where Muhammad was born.

Miracle   An amazing event which people believe was caused by God.

Muhammad   The Prophet who taught people about Islam.

Pilgrimage   A journey to a holy place. A person who goes on a pilgrimage is called a **pilgrim.**

Prophet   A person who receives messages from God.

Qur'an   The Muslim holy book.

Sacrifice   The killing of an animal as an offering to God.

Books to read

I am a Muslim by Manju Aggarwal (Franklin Watts, 1984)

Islam by Abdul Latif Al-Hoad (Wayland, 1986)

Islam for Children by Ahmad von Denffer (Islamic Foundation, 1981)

The Life of Muhammad by M. Davis (Wayland, 1987)

Index

Acknowledgements

The publisher would like to thank all those who provided pictures on the following pages: Camerapix Hutchison Library 4, 5, 11, 14, 17, 18, 24, 27, 28, 29, 30, 31, 32, 33, 34, 35, 39; Michael Holford 8; Hutchison Library cover; Mansell Collection 9; Christine Osborne 6, 7, 12, 13, 15, 16, 19, 20, 21, 22, 23, 25, 36, 37, 38, 41; Ann and Bury Peerless 40, 42, 43, 44; Wayland Library 10. The map on page 26 is by Malcolm Walker.